JULIA PROGRAM

BEYOND THE HORIZON OF STANDARD PRACTICES

OLIVER LUCAS JR

TABLE OF CONTENTS

Preface

Julia has captivated the hearts and minds of programmers seeking both elegance and performance. This language, born from a desire to have it all, has rapidly matured into a powerful tool for tackling complex problems across diverse domains. But with that growth comes a challenge: how do we move beyond the basics and truly master Julia's unique capabilities?

This book, "Julia Programming: Beyond the Horizon of Standard Practices," is your guide to unlocking the full potential of Julia. It's designed for those who have already tasted the power of Julia and are hungry for more. Whether you're a seasoned data scientist, a scientific researcher pushing the boundaries of computation, or a software engineer building high-performance applications, this book will equip you with the knowledge and techniques to write truly expert-level Julia code.

Within these pages, we'll delve into the depths of Julia's type system, master the art of metaprogramming, and explore advanced techniques for performance optimization. We'll uncover the secrets of parallel and distributed computing, learn how to extend Julia with custom features, and even venture into the exciting realms of GPU programming and quantum computing.

This is not just a book about *what* Julia can do, but *how* to do it with elegance, efficiency, and a deep understanding of the language's inner workings. We'll go beyond simple recipes and delve into the underlying principles, empowering you to make informed decisions and write code that is both powerful and maintainable.

Along the way, we'll emphasize best practices, community engagement, and the importance of contributing to the vibrant Julia ecosystem. By the time you reach the final page, you'll be well on your way to becoming a true Julia expert, ready to tackle the most challenging problems and contribute to the future of this exciting language.

So, join us on this journey beyond the horizon. Let's explore the depths of Julia together and unlock its full potential. The future of programming awaits!

Chapter 1

The Julia Zen

Mindset and Philosophy

1.1 Embracing Multiple Dispatch

Here's a breakdown of what "Embracing Multiple Dispatch" signifies in the context of our book:

A Paradigm Shift: For programmers coming from languages with single dispatch (like Python or Java), multiple dispatch represents a fundamental shift in how they approach code design. This subtitle emphasizes that Julia requires a new mindset, one that leverages the power and flexibility of dispatching methods based on the types of *all* arguments.

The Julia Advantage: Multiple dispatch is what sets Julia apart from many other languages. It enables code that is more generi extensible, and performant. By "embracing" it, readers will unlc the true potential of Julia and write code that is idiomatic a efficient.

Beyond the Basics: While the chapter will cover fundamentals of multiple dispatch, the subtitle implies further. It suggests exploring advanced techniques, patterns, and optimization strategies that rely on a understanding of this core concept.

A Foundation for Mastery: This chapter lays the groundwork for the entire book. By mastering multiple dispatch, readers will be equipped to tackle the more complex and specialized topics covered in later chapters.

In essence, "Embracing Multiple Dispatch" is a call to action. It encourages readers to fully engage with this powerful feature and make it an integral part of their Julia programming journey. It sets the stage for a book that delves into the depths of Julia, pushing the boundaries of what's possible with this high-performance language.

1.2 Type System Deep Dive

This subtitle signals that we're about to go beyond the introductory explanations of Julia's type system and really explore its intricacies. It promises a comprehensive and in-depth examination how types work in Julia, and how advanced users can leverage n for maximum effect.

what a "Deep Dive" into Julia's type system might entail:

the Basics: We'll move past simple type declarations and ncepts like:

t
c,
ck
and   s: How they define type hierarchies and enable

the   Understanding their role in performance and
going
design
deep   v to create flexible and reusable types with

Types: Expressing complex type

1

Type Aliases: Simplifying code and improving readability.

The Power of Types: We'll demonstrate how a deep understanding of the type system allows for:

Code Organization: Creating well-structured and maintainable code.

Performance Optimization: Leveraging type information for efficient code generation.

Error Detection: Catching errors at compile time rather than runtime.

Code Flexibility: Writing generic code that works with a variety of types.

Advanced Techniques: We'll delve into more sophisticated uses of the type system, such as:

Type Inference: Understanding how Julia infers types and how to influence it.

Reflection: Introspecting types and their properties at runtime.

Generated Functions: Using types to generate specialized code.

Traits: Defining and using traits to extend the type system.

Practical Applications: We'll show how to apply these concepts in real-world scenarios, like:

Building custom data structures.

Implementing efficient algorithms.

Designing robust APIs.

Extending Julia's functionality.

1.3 Metaprogramming Fundamentals

What is Metaprogramming?

We'll start with a clear definition of metaprogramming, emphasizing its unique ability to treat code as data. This will involve explaining how Julia code can be represented as an Abstract Syntax Tree (AST) and how this representation can be manipulated.

Core Concepts:

We'll introduce the essential building blocks of metaprogramming in Julia:

Macros: Explain how macros allow for code generation and manipulation before runtime, enabling powerful abstractions and domain-specific languages (DSLs).

Expressions: Illustrate how to work with code as data, constructing and manipulating expressions to generate new code dynamically.

Evaluation: Explore how Julia evaluates code, including how to control evaluation with `eval` and how to generate code that evaluates differently in different contexts.

Quote and Unquote: Demonstrate the mechanisms for escaping and evaluating code within macros, allowing for precise control over code generation.

Practical Examples:

We'll provide concrete examples of how metaprogramming can be used to:

Simplify repetitive code patterns.

Create custom language features.

Generate efficient code for specific tasks.

Extend Julia's syntax and functionality.

Building Blocks for Advanced Techniques:

We'll lay the groundwork for more advanced metaprogramming techniques covered later in the book, such as:

Domain-specific languages (DSLs).

Code analysis and transformation.

Compiler extensions.

Chapter 2

Performance as a First Principle

2.1 Profiling and Benchmarking

Profiling:

Understanding Profiling: We'll start by explaining what profiling is and why it's crucial for performance optimization. This will involve:

Different types of profiling: Introducing various profiling techniques (e.g., time-based, allocation-based, event-based) and their specific uses.

Julia's built-in profiler: Demonstrating how to use Julia's `Profile` module to analyze code execution and identify performance bottlenecks.

Visualizing profiling results: Exploring tools and techniques for visualizing profiling data, such as flame graphs and call graphs, to gain insights into code behavior.

Interpreting profiling data: Guiding readers on how to analyze profiling results, identify hotspots, and understand the reasons behind performance issues.

Benchmarking:

The Importance of Benchmarking: We'll explain why benchmarking is essential for measuring code performance and comparing different implementations. This will include:

Benchmarking methodologies: Introducing best practices for writing accurate and reliable benchmarks, including considerations for warm-up, statistical significance, and avoiding common pitfalls.

Julia's benchmarking tools: Showcasing tools like `@benchmark` and `BenchmarkTools.jl` for creating and running benchmarks, and analyzing their results.

Comparing performance: Demonstrating how to use benchmarking to compare different versions of code, algorithms, or libraries, and make informed decisions about optimization strategies.

Connecting Profiling and Benchmarking:

The Optimization Workflow: We'll illustrate how profiling and benchmarking work together in a performance optimization workflow. This involves:

Identifying bottlenecks with profiling: Using profiling to pinpoint areas of code that require optimization.

Measuring improvements with benchmarking: Employing benchmarking to quantify the impact of code changes and ensure that optimizations are effective.

Iterative optimization: Emphasizing the iterative nature of performance optimization, where profiling and benchmarking are used repeatedly to refine code and achieve optimal performance.

2.2 Memory Management and Allocation

Understanding Memory in Julia:

The Stack and the Heap: We'll start with a clear explanation of how Julia organizes memory, distinguishing between stack allocation (for local variables) and heap allocation (for dynamically sized data).

Value Types vs. Reference Types: We'll discuss the difference between value types (stored directly) and reference types (stored as pointers), and how this impacts memory usage and performance.

Garbage Collection: We'll explain how Julia's garbage collector (GC) works, including:

Generational GC: How Julia uses different generations to efficiently manage memory.

Mark-and-sweep: The basic algorithm behind Julia's GC.

Finalization: How objects are finalized before being reclaimed.

Optimizing Memory Allocation:

Reducing Allocations: We'll explore techniques for minimizing memory allocations, a key factor in achieving high performance. This includes:

Pre-allocation: Allocating memory upfront for arrays and other data structures to avoid repeated allocations.

Stack allocation: Encouraging the use of stack allocation whenever possible to reduce GC pressure.

Reusing memory: Techniques like in-place operations and object pools to avoid unnecessary allocations.

Managing Memory Layout: We'll discuss how data structures and memory layout can impact performance. This includes:

Array ordering: Understanding how row-major and column-major ordering affect memory access patterns.

Data locality: Improving performance by keeping related data close together in memory.

Struct layout: Optimizing the arrangement of fields within structs for efficient memory access.

Tools and Techniques:

Memory profiling tools: We'll introduce tools and techniques for analyzing memory usage and identifying memory leaks. This includes:

Profiling memory allocations: Using tools to track memory allocations and identify areas of code that allocate excessively.

Detecting memory leaks: Techniques for finding and fixing memory leaks that can lead to performance degradation and crashes.

Advanced memory management: We'll touch on more advanced topics like:

Manual memory management: Exploring Julia's low-level memory management functions for specialized use cases.

Weak references: Understanding how weak references can be used to avoid memory leaks.

2.3 Optimizing for Speed and Efficiency

Code-Level Optimizations:

Writing Efficient Code: We'll start with fundamental principles of writing efficient Julia code, including:

Avoiding unnecessary allocations: Minimizing the creation of temporary objects to reduce garbage collection overhead.

Loop optimization: Techniques for writing efficient loops, such as vectorization, loop fusion, and avoiding unnecessary bounds checks.

Function specialization: Leveraging Julia's type system and multiple dispatch to generate specialized code for different types.

In-place operations: Modifying data structures directly to avoid creating copies.

Using the right data structures: Choosing the most efficient data structures for the task at hand.

Compiler Optimizations:

Understanding the Julia Compiler: We'll provide insights into how the Julia compiler works and how to write code that the compiler can optimize effectively. This includes:

Type stability: Writing functions that always return the same type to enable compiler optimizations.

Code inlining: Understanding when and how the compiler inlines functions to reduce function call overhead.

Avoiding dynamic dispatch: Minimizing the use of dynamic dispatch in performance-critical sections of code.

Performance Measurement and Analysis:

Benchmarking and Profiling: We'll reiterate the importance of benchmarking to measure performance and profiling to identify bottlenecks, emphasizing their role in the optimization process.

Performance Analysis Tools: Introducing additional tools and techniques for analyzing performance, such as:

Tracing: Tracking the execution of code to identify performance issues.

Flame graphs: Visualizing the call stack and execution time of functions.

Performance counters: Monitoring hardware performance metrics to identify bottlenecks.

Advanced Optimization Techniques:

Parallel Computing: Exploring techniques for leveraging multiple cores or processors to speed up computations, including:

Multithreading: Using threads to execute code concurrently.

Distributed computing: Distributing computations across multiple machines.

Memory Management: Revisiting memory management techniques for optimizing performance, such as:

Data locality: Arranging data in memory to improve cache utilization.

Memory alignment: Aligning data structures to improve memory access speed.

Metaprogramming: Leveraging metaprogramming techniques to generate optimized code.

Chapter 3

Beyond the REPL: Building Robust Applications

3.1 Package Development and Distribution

Creating a Package:

The Anatomy of a Julia Package: We'll start by explaining the structure of a Julia package, including:

Project initialization: Using the `Pkg` REPL mode or the `PkgTemplates.jl` package to generate a basic package structure.

Key files and directories: Understanding the roles of `Project.toml` and `Manifest.toml` for dependency management, and the `src` directory for source code.

Module structure: Organizing code into modules and submodules for clarity and maintainability.

Developing Package Code:

Writing Testable Code: Emphasizing the importance of writing unit tests and demonstrating how to use Julia's testing framework.

Documenting Your Package: Explaining how to write clear and comprehensive documentation using Documenter.jl, including docstrings, examples, and tutorials.

Versioning and Releases: Introducing semantic versioning and best practices for managing package versions and releases.

Distributing Your Package:

Registering Your Package: Guiding readers through the process of registering their package with the General registry, making it available to the Julia community.

Publishing to the Registry: Explaining how to tag and release new versions of the package to the registry.

Managing Dependencies: Understanding how to declare and manage dependencies on other packages, including specifying version ranges and compatibility.

Advanced Package Development:

Building Complex Packages: Exploring techniques for building more complex packages, such as:

Developing packages with binary dependencies.

Creating packages that interface with external libraries.

Building packages that provide custom Julia extensions.

Continuous Integration and Deployment: Setting up automated testing and deployment workflows using tools like GitHub Actions.

Package Best Practices: Sharing best practices for package development, including code style, documentation, and community engagement.

3.2 Testing and Debugging Strategies

Testing in Julia:

Types of Testing: We'll introduce different testing methodologies relevant to Julia, including:

Unit Testing: Testing individual functions and modules in isolation to ensure they work as expected.

Integration Testing: Testing how different parts of the application work together.

Property-Based Testing: Defining properties that should hold true for a function and generating test cases automatically.

Test-Driven Development (TDD): Writing tests before writing code to guide development and ensure code correctness from the start.

Testing Frameworks and Tools: We'll explore Julia's testing ecosystem, including:

`Test` **standard library:** Demonstrating how to use the built-in `Test` module for writing and running tests.

`ReTest`**:** Introducing ReTest for running tests and analyzing their results.

Test-driven development packages: Exploring packages like `FactCheck.jl` and `ReferenceTests.jl` that support property-based testing and other advanced testing techniques.

Debugging in Julia:

Debugging Techniques: We'll cover various debugging strategies, including:

Print Debugging: Using `println` statements to inspect values and track program execution.

The Debugger: Introducing Julia's built-in debugger and demonstrating how to set breakpoints, step through code, and inspect variables.

Debugging Tools: Exploring tools like Debugger.jl, Juno's debugger, and VS Code's debugger for enhanced debugging capabilities.

Static Analysis: Using tools like Lint.jl to identify potential code issues before runtime.

Effective Debugging Strategies:

Understanding Error Messages: We'll guide readers on how to interpret Julia's error messages and use them to identify the root cause of problems.

Isolating the Issue: Techniques for narrowing down the source of errors, such as using binary search or commenting out code.

Testing Hypotheses: Formulating hypotheses about the cause of errors and designing tests to confirm or refute them.

Logging and Tracing: Using logging and tracing to track program execution and identify unexpected behavior.

Best Practices:

Writing Testable Code: Emphasizing the importance of writing code that is easy to test, such as using small functions, clear interfaces, and dependency injection.

Debugging Workflow: Establishing a systematic debugging workflow to efficiently identify and resolve issues.

Common Debugging Pitfalls: Addressing common debugging challenges and how to avoid them.

3.3 Documentation and Code Style

Documentation in Julia:

Why Document? We'll start by emphasizing the benefits of good documentation, including:

Improved Code Understanding: Making code easier to understand for both the original author and other developers.

Reduced Maintenance Costs: Helping future developers (including your future self!) quickly grasp the purpose and functionality of code.

Facilitating Collaboration: Enabling effective teamwork by providing clear explanations and usage examples.

Generating Documentation: Using tools like Documenter.jl to automatically generate documentation websites from code comments.

Types of Documentation: We'll explore different levels of documentation:

Inline Comments: Using comments within code to explain complex logic, algorithms, or design decisions.

Docstrings: Writing structured documentation for modules, functions, and types using docstrings, which can be processed by documentation generators.

Tutorials and Examples: Creating comprehensive guides and examples to demonstrate how to use the code effectively.

README files: Providing an overview of the project, its purpose, and how to get started.

Code Style in Julia:

The Importance of Style: We'll discuss why consistent code style is essential for maintainability and collaboration.

Julia Style Guide: We'll introduce the official Julia style guide and highlight its key recommendations, including:

Naming conventions: Guidelines for naming variables, functions, and types.

Indentation and spacing: Rules for consistent formatting to improve readability.

Code organization: Best practices for structuring code into modules and files.

Comment style: Recommendations for writing clear and informative comments.

Code Formatting Tools: We'll explore tools that can help enforce code style and automate formatting, such as:

JuliaFormatter.jl: A popular package for automatically formatting Julia code.

Lint.jl: A tool for static code analysis that can identify style violations and potential code issues.

Best Practices:

Writing Clear and Concise Documentation: Emphasizing the importance of writing documentation that is easy to understand and focused on the needs of the user.

Keeping Documentation Up-to-Date: Stressing the need to update documentation whenever code changes to avoid inconsistencies and confusion.

Using a Consistent Code Style: Encouraging the adoption of a consistent style guide to improve code readability and maintainability.

Documenting Design Decisions: Explaining the rationale behind design choices to help future developers understand the codebase.

Chapter 4

Metaprogramming Mastery

4.1 Macros and Code Generation

Understanding Macros:

What are Macros? We'll start with a clear explanation of what macros are and how they differ from regular functions. This will involve:

Code as Data: Emphasizing that macros operate on code as data, represented by Julia's Abstract Syntax Tree (AST).

Compile-Time Execution: Explaining that macros are executed at compile time, allowing them to generate and manipulate code before the program runs.

Hygienic Macros: Introducing Julia's hygienic macro system, which helps prevent unintended variable capture and ensures code clarity.

Macro Syntax and Usage:

Defining Macros: We'll cover the syntax for defining macros using the `macro` keyword and the @ prefix for macro calls.

Macro Arguments: Explaining how to pass arguments to macros and how to manipulate them within the macro definition.

Code Generation: Demonstrating how to use macros to generate Julia code dynamically, including:

String Manipulation: Using string interpolation and other techniques to construct code strings.

Expression Manipulation: Working with Julia expressions to create and modify code structures.

Quote and Unquote: Mastering the use of `quote` and `unquote` to control code evaluation within macros.

Advanced Macro Techniques:

Macro Hygiene: Delving deeper into macro hygiene and how to avoid common pitfalls.

Recursive Macros: Exploring how to define macros that call themselves, enabling powerful code generation patterns.

Macros and DSLs: Illustrating how macros can be used to create domain-specific languages (DSLs) that extend Julia's syntax and functionality.

Introspection and Reflection: Using macros to inspect and manipulate code at compile time, enabling advanced metaprogramming techniques.

Practical Examples and Use Cases:

Simplifying Repetitive Code: Showing how macros can eliminate boilerplate code and reduce code duplication.

Creating Custom Language Features: Demonstrating how to use macros to add new syntax or features to the Julia language.

Generating Optimized Code: Exploring how macros can be used to generate specialized code for specific tasks or data structures.

Analyzing and Transforming Code: Using macros to analyze code and perform transformations at compile time.

4.2 Domain-Specific Languages (DSLs)

What are DSLs?

Defining DSLs: We'll start by clearly defining what DSLs are and how they differ from general-purpose languages (GPLs). This will involve:

Specialized Syntax: Highlighting that DSLs have their own syntax optimized for a specific domain or task.

Increased Abstraction: Explaining how DSLs allow developers to express solutions at a higher level of abstraction, closer to the problem domain.

Improved Readability and Maintainability: Demonstrating how DSLs can make code more concise, readable, and easier to maintain.

Building DSLs in Julia:

Leveraging Macros: We'll explain how Julia's macro system provides a powerful mechanism for creating DSLs. This includes:

Syntax Manipulation: Using macros to define custom syntax rules and parse DSL code.

Code Generation: Employing macros to translate DSL code into Julia code that can be executed.

Example DSLs: Showcasing existing DSLs in Julia, such as those used for querying databases, defining mathematical expressions, or specifying build systems.

Designing Effective DSLs:

Domain Analysis: Emphasizing the importance of carefully analyzing the target domain to identify the key concepts and operations that the DSL should support.

Syntax Design: Choosing an appropriate syntax that is concise, readable, and intuitive for users of the DSL.

Abstraction Level: Finding the right balance between abstraction and expressiveness to make the DSL easy to use without sacrificing functionality.

Error Handling: Implementing robust error handling mechanisms to provide helpful feedback to users.

Advanced DSL Techniques:

Composable DSLs: Exploring how to create DSLs that can be combined and extended to support more complex scenarios.

Embedded DSLs: Creating DSLs that are tightly integrated with Julia's syntax and semantics.

External DSLs: Developing DSLs with their own parsers and grammars for maximum flexibility.

Practical Examples and Use Cases:

Data Manipulation and Querying: Building DSLs for working with data, such as querying databases or performing data transformations.

Mathematical Modeling and Simulation: Creating DSLs for defining mathematical models and running simulations.

Configuration and Build Systems: Developing DSLs for specifying configuration parameters or automating build processes.

Graphics and Visualization: Designing DSLs for creating visualizations and interactive graphics.

4.3 Extending Julia with Custom Features

Methods for Extension:

Multiple Dispatch: Reiterating how multiple dispatch is the cornerstone of extensibility in Julia. We'll show how to define new methods for existing functions to handle custom types or add new behaviors.

Metaprogramming with Macros: Revisiting macros and demonstrating how they can be used to introduce new syntax, define custom operators, or even create entirely new control flow constructs.

Generated Functions: Exploring how to generate specialized functions at compile time based on type information or other criteria, enabling highly optimized code for specific scenarios.

Extending Core Functionality:

Adding New Types: Demonstrating how to define new types that integrate seamlessly with Julia's type system, including abstract types, concrete types, and parametric types.

Overloading Operators: Showing how to overload existing operators (like +, *, or ==) to work with custom types, allowing for more natural and expressive code.

Creating Custom Iterators: Explaining how to define new iterator types that conform to Julia's iteration protocols, enabling custom iteration patterns for specific data structures or algorithms.

Advanced Extension Techniques:

Compiler Plugins: Introducing the concept of compiler plugins, which allow developers to hook into the Julia compiler and modify its behavior. This can be used for tasks like:

Code analysis and transformation: Analyzing and modifying code at compile time to optimize performance or enforce coding standards.

Custom code generation: Generating specialized code based on specific conditions or annotations.

Language extensions: Introducing new language features or syntax.

Examples and Use Cases:

Domain-Specific Languages (DSLs): Revisiting DSLs and showing how they can be used to extend Julia's syntax and semantics for specific domains.

Performance Optimization: Using custom features to optimize performance for specific tasks or hardware architectures.

Code Analysis and Debugging: Developing tools for code analysis, debugging, or testing that leverage custom extensions.

Scientific Computing: Creating specialized types and functions for scientific computing tasks, such as linear algebra, differential equations, or numerical simulations.

Considerations and Best Practices:

Maintaining Compatibility: Emphasizing the importance of designing extensions that are compatible with existing Julia code and libraries.

Avoiding Name Conflicts: Strategies for avoiding name conflicts with existing functions or types.

Documentation and Testing: Highlighting the importance of documenting and testing custom features to ensure their usability and reliability.

Chapter 5

Parallel and Distributed Computing

5.1 Multithreading and Asynchronous Programming

Multithreading in Julia:

Threads and Parallelism: We'll start by explaining the concept of threads and how they enable parallel execution on multiple cores.

Julia's Threading Model: We'll introduce Julia's threading model, including:

Shared Memory: Explaining that threads share the same memory space, which allows for efficient communication but requires careful synchronization to avoid race conditions.

Task-Based Parallelism: Describing how Julia uses tasks to schedule and manage threads.

Data Races and Synchronization: Discussing the challenges of data races and how to use synchronization primitives like locks, atomic operations, and condition variables to ensure thread safety.

Asynchronous Programming in Julia:

Non-Blocking Operations: We'll explain the concept of asynchronous programming and how it allows programs to perform operations without blocking the main thread.

Tasks and Coroutines: Introducing Julia's `Task` type and how it can be used to create coroutines that can be scheduled and executed concurrently.

`async`/`await` **Syntax:** Demonstrating how to use the `async` and `await` keywords to write asynchronous code that is easy to read and reason about.

Channels: Explaining how to use channels for communication and synchronization between tasks.

Combining Multithreading and Asynchronous Programming:

Parallel I/O Operations: Showing how to use asynchronous programming to perform I/O-bound tasks concurrently, such as reading from files or making network requests.

Multithreaded Algorithms: Exploring how to design algorithms that can be executed in parallel using multiple threads.

Task Scheduling and Management: Discussing strategies for managing tasks and scheduling them efficiently across multiple threads.

Advanced Techniques and Considerations:

Thread Pools: Introducing the concept of thread pools and how they can be used to manage threads more efficiently.

Race Condition Detection: Exploring tools and techniques for detecting and preventing race conditions in multithreaded code.

Performance Optimization: Discussing strategies for optimizing multithreaded and asynchronous code for maximum performance.

Debugging Concurrent Code: Addressing the challenges of debugging concurrent code and introducing tools and techniques for identifying and resolving concurrency-related issues.

Practical Examples and Use Cases:

Concurrent Web Servers: Building web servers that can handle multiple requests concurrently using asynchronous programming and multithreading.

Parallel Data Processing: Processing large datasets in parallel using multithreaded algorithms.

Real-time Applications: Developing real-time applications that require responsive and non-blocking behavior.

5.2 Distributed Computing with Julia

Fundamentals of Distributed Computing:

Why Distribute? We'll start by explaining the motivations for distributed computing, including:

Increased Computational Power: Harnessing the combined resources of multiple machines to solve larger and more complex problems.

Improved Scalability: Distributing workload to handle growing datasets or increasing user demand.

Fault Tolerance: Designing systems that can continue operating even if some machines fail.

Distributed Architectures: We'll introduce common distributed computing architectures, such as:

Client-server: A central server provides services to multiple clients.

Peer-to-peer: Machines communicate and collaborate directly with each other.

Cloud computing: Utilizing resources from a cloud provider.

Julia's Distributed Computing Model:

Processes and Communication: We'll explain how Julia's distributed computing model is built on:

Multiple Processes: Launching separate Julia processes on different machines.

Message Passing: Using message passing for communication and data exchange between processes.

Remote References: Introducing `Future` and `RemoteChannel` for referring to objects on remote processes.

Remote Calls: Using `@spawnat` and `remotecall` to execute functions on remote processes.

Tools and Techniques:

ClusterManagers.jl: Introducing `ClusterManagers.jl` for managing and interacting with clusters of Julia processes.

DistributedArrays.jl: Exploring `DistributedArrays.jl` for creating and manipulating arrays that are distributed across multiple processes.

SharedArrays.jl: Discussing `SharedArrays.jl` for sharing data between processes on the same machine using shared memory.

Parallel Computing Tools: Revisiting tools like `@distributed` for parallel loops and reductions that can be extended to distributed environments.

Advanced Distributed Computing:

Distributed Algorithms: Exploring algorithms specifically designed for distributed environments, such as distributed sorting, searching, and graph algorithms.

Fault Tolerance: Discussing strategies for handling failures in distributed systems, such as checkpointing and replication.

Performance Optimization: Addressing performance considerations in distributed computing, including communication overhead, data locality, and load balancing.

Debugging Distributed Code: Introducing tools and techniques for debugging code running in a distributed environment.

Practical Examples and Use Cases:

Distributed Machine Learning: Training machine learning models on large datasets distributed across multiple machines.

Scientific Simulations: Running large-scale scientific simulations that require significant computational resources.

Data-Intensive Applications: Processing and analyzing massive datasets distributed across a cluster.

Financial Modeling: Performing complex financial simulations and risk analysis in a distributed environment..

5.3 High-Performance Computing (HPC) Applications

Julia for HPC:

Why Julia for HPC? We'll start by highlighting Julia's advantages for HPC, including:

High Performance: Demonstrating how Julia's just-in-time (JIT) compilation and type system enable performance comparable to C or Fortran.

Parallelism: Revisiting Julia's rich support for parallelism, including multithreading, distributed computing, and GPU programming.

Ease of Use: Emphasizing that Julia's high-level syntax and dynamic nature make it easier to develop and maintain complex HPC applications compared to traditional low-level languages.

Rich Ecosystem: Showcasing Julia's growing ecosystem of packages for scientific computing, numerical analysis, and data visualization.

HPC Application Domains:

Scientific Simulations: Exploring how Julia can be used for:

Climate Modeling: Simulating climate patterns and predicting future changes.

Fluid Dynamics: Modeling fluid flow in various applications, such as aircraft design or weather forecasting.

Molecular Dynamics: Simulating the interactions of atoms and molecules to understand material properties or drug interactions.

Astrophysics: Simulating the evolution of stars, galaxies, and the universe.

Data-Intensive Computing: Discussing how Julia can handle:

Genomics: Analyzing large genomic datasets to understand diseases and develop new treatments.

High Energy Physics: Processing and analyzing data from particle accelerators.

Financial Modeling: Performing complex financial simulations and risk analysis.

Image and Signal Processing: Analyzing large images and signals from sources like satellites or medical devices.

HPC Tools and Techniques:

Parallel Computing: Revisiting and expanding on Julia's parallel computing capabilities, including:

DistributedArrays.jl: Distributing large arrays across multiple processes or machines.

MPI.jl: Integrating with the Message Passing Interface (MPI) for high-performance communication in distributed environments.

CUDA.jl: Programming GPUs for accelerated computations.

Performance Optimization: Addressing performance considerations specific to HPC, such as:

Memory Management: Optimizing memory usage and data locality for large-scale computations.

Profiling and Benchmarking: Using profiling tools to identify performance bottlenecks and benchmarking to measure improvements.

Code Optimization: Applying advanced code optimization techniques to improve performance on specific hardware architectures.

Examples and Case Studies:

Celeste.jl: Showcasing Celeste.jl, a Julia package used for analyzing astronomical data to identify stars and galaxies.

Oceananigans.jl: Presenting Oceananigans.jl, a Julia package for simulating ocean currents and fluid dynamics.

Climate Modeling: Highlighting Julia's use in climate modeling projects, such as the CliMA project.

Bioinformatics: Exploring Julia's applications in bioinformatics, such as genomic analysis and drug discovery.

Chapter 6

Interfacing with the External World

6.1 C and Fortran Interoperability

Why C and Fortran Interoperability?

Legacy Code: We'll start by acknowledging the vast amount of existing C and Fortran code in scientific computing, engineering, and other fields. Interoperability allows Julia to tap into these resources and build upon them.

Performance: C and Fortran are known for their performance, especially in computationally intensive tasks. Interoperating with them can provide access to highly optimized libraries or functions.

Specialized Libraries: Many specialized libraries, particularly in areas like linear algebra, signal processing, and numerical analysis, are written in C or Fortran. Interoperability enables Julia to utilize these libraries directly.

Interoperating with C:

`ccall`: We'll introduce `ccall`, Julia's primary mechanism for calling C functions. This will involve:

Function Signatures: Explaining how to specify the C function's name, library, return type, and argument types in Julia.

Data Type Mapping: Discussing how Julia data types map to C data types and how to handle pointers and structures.

Memory Management: Addressing memory management considerations when passing data between Julia and C.

`cfunction`: We'll cover `cfunction`, which allows defining Julia functions that can be called from C.

Interoperating with Fortran:

Fortran Calling Conventions: Explaining the differences in calling conventions between Julia and Fortran, including argument passing and array ordering.

`ccall` **for Fortran:** Demonstrating how to use `ccall` to call Fortran subroutines and functions.

Wrapper Libraries: Discussing the use of wrapper libraries to simplify Fortran interoperability, such as `FortranFiles.jl` for reading and writing Fortran data files.

Advanced Interoperability Techniques:

C++ Interoperability: Touching on how to interact with C++ code, although with the caveat that it can be more complex due to C++'s object-oriented nature.

Building C/Fortran Libraries: Explaining how to build C and Fortran libraries that can be used from Julia.

Debugging Interoperability Code: Addressing the challenges of debugging code that involves interactions between different languages.

Practical Examples and Use Cases:

Calling BLAS and LAPACK: Demonstrating how to call functions from BLAS and LAPACK, widely used linear algebra libraries written in Fortran.

Accessing Hardware APIs: Using C interoperability to access hardware APIs or device drivers.

Integrating with Existing C/Fortran Codebases: Showing how to integrate Julia code with existing C or Fortran projects.

Building Hybrid Applications: Creating applications that combine the strengths of Julia, C, and Fortran.

6.2 Working with Databases and APIs

Databases:

Why Use Databases? We'll start by explaining the benefits of using databases for managing data, including:

Persistence: Storing data reliably and making it accessible even after the program terminates.

Organization: Structuring data efficiently for easy retrieval and manipulation.

Scalability: Handling large amounts of data and supporting concurrent access by multiple users.

Data Integrity: Ensuring data consistency and accuracy through mechanisms like transactions and constraints.

Database Types: We'll introduce different types of databases, including:

Relational Databases: Structured data organized in tables with rows and columns (e.g., MySQL, PostgreSQL).

NoSQL Databases: Flexible schema-less databases for unstructured or semi-structured data (e.g., MongoDB, Cassandra).

Working with Databases in Julia:

Database Drivers: Introducing Julia packages that provide database drivers for connecting to various database systems.

Querying and Manipulating Data: Demonstrating how to execute SQL queries to retrieve, insert, update, and delete data.

Object-Relational Mapping (ORM): Exploring ORM techniques for mapping database tables to Julia objects.

APIs:

What are APIs? We'll explain the concept of APIs (Application Programming Interfaces) as a way for different software systems to communicate and exchange data.

API Types: Introducing different types of APIs, such as:

REST APIs: APIs that use HTTP requests to access and manipulate resources.

GraphQL APIs: APIs that allow clients to request specific data.

Working with APIs in Julia:

HTTP Clients: Introducing Julia packages for making HTTP requests to interact with APIs.

JSON Handling: Demonstrating how to parse and generate JSON data, a common format for API communication.

API Wrappers: Exploring Julia packages that provide convenient wrappers for popular APIs.

Connecting Databases and APIs:

Building Data-Driven Applications: Illustrating how to combine database and API interactions to create applications that:

Retrieve data from APIs and store it in databases.

Expose data from databases through APIs.

Create applications that interact with both databases and APIs.

Advanced Topics:

Asynchronous API Calls: Using asynchronous programming to make API calls without blocking the main thread.

API Authentication and Authorization: Implementing secure authentication and authorization mechanisms for API access.

Database Transactions: Ensuring data consistency and integrity using database transactions.

Data Serialization: Exploring different data serialization formats for API communication.

Practical Examples and Use Cases:

Building a Web Application: Creating a web application that interacts with a database to store and retrieve user data and uses APIs to access external services.

Data Analysis and Visualization: Retrieving data from APIs, storing it in a database, and then analyzing and visualizing it using Julia's data science tools.

Financial Modeling: Accessing financial data through APIs, storing it in a database, and performing financial modeling and analysis.

Social Media Analysis: Collecting data from social media APIs, storing it in a database, and performing sentiment analysis or network analysis.

6.3 Building Web Applications with Julia

Why Julia for Web Development?

Performance: We'll start by highlighting Julia's speed and efficiency, which can be crucial for handling demanding web applications with high traffic or complex computations.

Productivity: Julia's high-level syntax and dynamic nature can lead to faster development and easier maintenance compared to some traditional web development languages.

Flexibility: Julia's versatility allows for building various types of web applications, from simple APIs to interactive data dashboards and real-time applications.

Ecosystem: We'll introduce Julia's growing ecosystem of web frameworks and packages that simplify web development.

Web Frameworks:

Genie.jl: We'll focus on Genie.jl, a full-featured web framework that provides:

MVC Architecture: Organizing code into models, views, and controllers for maintainability and scalability.

Routing: Defining URL routes and handling HTTP requests.

Templating: Generating dynamic HTML content using templates.

Database Integration: Connecting to databases and managing data persistence.

Security Features: Implementing authentication, authorization, and other security measures.

Other Frameworks: We'll briefly mention other web frameworks like:

HTTP.jl: A lower-level framework for building custom web servers and APIs.

Mux.jl: A flexible routing library for building web applications.

Dash.jl: A framework for building reactive dashboards and data visualization applications.

Building Web Applications:

Setting up a Development Environment: Guiding readers through setting up a web development environment with Julia, including installing necessary packages and configuring a web server.

Creating a Simple Web Application: Starting with a basic "Hello, world!" web application to illustrate fundamental concepts like routing and templating.

Handling User Input: Demonstrating how to handle user input from forms, process data, and generate dynamic responses.

Working with Databases: Connecting to a database and performing CRUD (Create, Read, Update, Delete) operations on data.

Building REST APIs: Creating APIs that can be accessed by other applications using HTTP requests.

Deploying Web Applications: Explaining how to deploy Julia web applications to cloud platforms or web servers.

Advanced Topics:

WebSockets: Using WebSockets for real-time communication between the server and client.

Asynchronous Programming: Leveraging asynchronous programming to handle concurrent requests and improve performance.

Security Best Practices: Implementing security measures to protect web applications from common vulnerabilities.

Frontend Integration: Integrating Julia web applications with frontend frameworks like React or Vue.js.

Practical Examples and Use Cases:

Interactive Data Dashboards: Building dashboards that visualize data from databases or APIs, allowing users to explore and interact with the data.

Real-time Applications: Creating applications that provide real-time updates, such as chat applications or live data monitoring tools.

Scientific Web Applications: Developing web applications that perform scientific computations or simulations and display results interactively.

Machine Learning APIs: Deploying machine learning models as web services that can be accessed through APIs.

Chapter 7

Advanced Data Science and Machine Learning

7.1 Building Custom Machine Learning Models

Why Build Custom Models?

Unique Problems: We'll start by emphasizing that not all problems can be solved effectively with off-the-shelf models. Custom models allow us to address specific challenges and datasets that might not fit well with existing solutions.

Deeper Understanding: Building custom models fosters a deeper understanding of the underlying algorithms and principles of machine learning.

Flexibility and Control: Custom models provide greater flexibility and control over the model's architecture, parameters, and training process.

Innovation: Creating custom models opens the door to developing novel approaches and pushing the boundaries of machine learning.

Fundamentals of Custom Model Building:

Machine Learning Basics: We'll briefly review fundamental concepts like:

Supervised, Unsupervised, and Reinforcement Learning: Different types of machine learning tasks.

Model Training and Evaluation: The process of training a model on data and evaluating its performance.

Common Algorithms: An overview of common machine learning algorithms (e.g., linear regression, decision trees, neural networks).

Julia's Machine Learning Ecosystem: We'll introduce key packages for building custom models:

Flux.jl: A powerful and flexible framework for building neural networks.

MLJ.jl: A machine learning toolbox that provides a unified interface for various algorithms and model building tasks.

Knet.jl: A deep learning framework with GPU support.

Building Custom Models with Flux.jl:

Neural Network Basics: We'll cover the basics of neural networks, including layers, activation functions, and backpropagation.

Defining Model Architectures: Demonstrating how to define custom neural network architectures using Flux.jl's layers and functions.

Training and Optimization: Explaining how to train models using different optimizers, loss functions, and regularization techniques.

Working with Data: Loading and preprocessing data for model training and evaluation.

Beyond Neural Networks:

Other Model Types: Exploring other types of custom models, such as:

Decision Trees and Random Forests: Building custom tree-based models for classification or regression.

Support Vector Machines (SVMs): Implementing custom SVMs for classification tasks.

Clustering Algorithms: Creating custom clustering algorithms for unsupervised learning.

Advanced Techniques:

Model Interpretability: Discussing techniques for understanding and interpreting the behavior of custom models.

Hyperparameter Tuning: Exploring methods for optimizing model hyperparameters to achieve the best performance.

Model Deployment: Deploying custom models as web services or integrating them into other applications.

Practical Examples and Use Cases:

Image Recognition: Building a custom image recognition model using convolutional neural networks.

Natural Language Processing: Creating a custom sentiment analysis model using recurrent neural networks.

Time Series Forecasting: Developing a custom time series forecasting model for predicting future values.

Anomaly Detection: Implementing a custom anomaly detection model to identify unusual patterns in data.

7.2 Deep Learning with Julia

Why Julia for Deep Learning?

Performance: We'll reiterate Julia's speed advantages, which are crucial for training computationally intensive deep learning models.

Automatic Differentiation: Highlighting Julia's excellent automatic differentiation capabilities (with packages like Zygote.jl) that simplify gradient calculations, a core component of deep learning.

GPU Support: Emphasizing Julia's ability to leverage GPUs for accelerated deep learning training with packages like CUDA.jl.

Flexibility: Julia's dynamic nature allows for easy experimentation with different model architectures and training techniques.

Ecosystem: Introducing Julia's deep learning ecosystem, including frameworks like Flux.jl and Knet.jl, and packages for data loading, preprocessing, and visualization.

Deep Learning Fundamentals:

Neural Networks: Reviewing the basics of neural networks, including:

Layers: Different types of layers (dense, convolutional, recurrent) and their roles in a network.

Activation Functions: Non-linear functions that introduce complexity and allow neural networks to learn complex patterns.

Backpropagation: The algorithm used to calculate gradients and update model weights during training.

Deep Learning Architectures: Exploring popular deep learning architectures:

Convolutional Neural Networks (CNNs): For image recognition, object detection, and other image-related tasks.

Recurrent Neural Networks (RNNs): For natural language processing, time series analysis, and sequential data.

Generative Adversarial Networks (GANs): For generating new data that resembles the training data.

Building Deep Learning Models with Flux.jl:

Model Construction: Demonstrating how to construct deep learning models using Flux.jl's layers and functions.

Training and Optimization: Explaining how to train deep learning models using optimizers, loss functions, and regularization techniques.

Data Loading and Preprocessing: Using Julia packages to load and preprocess data for deep learning training.

GPU Acceleration: Leveraging GPUs to speed up training with CUDA.jl.

Advanced Deep Learning Topics:

Transfer Learning: Utilizing pre-trained models to accelerate training or improve performance on new tasks.

Deep Reinforcement Learning: Exploring deep reinforcement learning techniques for training agents to interact with environments.

Model Interpretability: Understanding and interpreting the decisions made by deep learning models.

Deployment: Deploying deep learning models as web services or integrating them into other applications.

Practical Examples and Use Cases:

Image Classification: Building a CNN to classify images into different categories.

Object Detection: Training a model to detect objects within images.

Natural Language Processing: Creating a RNN for sentiment analysis or machine translation.

Time Series Forecasting: Developing a deep learning model for predicting future values in time series data.

7.3 Data Visualization and Exploration

Why Visualize and Explore?

Understanding Data: We'll start by emphasizing that visualization is key to understanding complex datasets. It allows us to:

Identify Patterns: Spot trends, outliers, and relationships that might not be apparent from raw data.

Uncover Insights: Gain a deeper understanding of the data and extract meaningful information.

Communicate Findings: Present data in a clear and compelling way to share insights with others.

Support Decision-Making: Use visualizations to inform data-driven decisions.

Exploration Techniques: We'll introduce various data exploration techniques, including:

Summary Statistics: Calculating basic statistics (mean, median, standard deviation) to get a sense of the data distribution.

Data Wrangling: Cleaning, transforming, and preparing data for visualization.

Dimensionality Reduction: Reducing the number of variables to make complex data easier to visualize and analyze.

Visualization Tools in Julia:

Plots.jl: We'll focus on Plots.jl, a versatile and powerful plotting library that provides:

Variety of Plot Types: Creating various plots, including line plots, scatter plots, bar charts, histograms, heatmaps, and more.

Customization: Customizing plot appearance with colors, labels, legends, and annotations.

Interactive Plots: Generating interactive plots that allow users to zoom, pan, and explore data.

Backends: Supporting different plotting backends (GR, PyPlot, Plotly) for flexibility and diverse output options.

Other Visualization Tools: We'll mention other visualization packages like:

Makie.jl: A high-performance plotting library with advanced 3D visualization capabilities.

Gadfly.jl: A grammar of graphics-based plotting package for creating publication-quality visualizations.

Creating Effective Visualizations:

Choosing the Right Plot Type: Guiding readers on selecting appropriate plot types based on the data and the message they want to convey.

Visual Design Principles: Introducing basic visual design principles, such as:

Clarity: Ensuring visualizations are easy to understand and interpret.

Accuracy: Representing data accurately and avoiding misleading visualizations.

Aesthetics: Creating visually appealing and engaging visualizations.

Data Exploration Workflow:

Data Loading and Preprocessing: Loading data from various sources and preparing it for visualization.

Exploratory Data Analysis (EDA): Using visualizations and summary statistics to explore data and identify patterns.

Data Storytelling: Creating a narrative with visualizations to communicate insights effectively.

Practical Examples and Use Cases:

Analyzing Time Series Data: Visualizing time series data to identify trends, seasonality, and anomalies.

Exploring Relationships: Using scatter plots, heatmaps, and correlation matrices to examine relationships between variables.

Comparing Groups: Creating bar charts, box plots, and violin plots to compare different groups or categories.

Visualizing Geographic Data: Plotting data on maps to understand spatial patterns and distributions.

Chapter 8

Scientific Computing and Simulations

8.1 Numerical Methods and Algorithms

Why Numerical Methods?

Limitations of Analytical Solutions: We'll start by explaining that many real-world problems involve complex equations or systems that cannot be solved exactly using analytical methods.

Approximations: Numerical methods provide approximate solutions with a controlled level of accuracy, making them essential for solving a wide range of scientific and engineering problems.

Julia's Strengths: We'll highlight how Julia's performance, ease of use, and extensive mathematical libraries make it an ideal language for implementing and applying numerical methods.

Core Numerical Methods:

Root Finding: Finding the roots (zeros) of functions, including:

Bisection Method: A simple and robust method for finding roots in a given interval.

Newton-Raphson Method: A faster method that uses the derivative of the function.

Secant Method: An approximation of Newton-Raphson that doesn't require the derivative.

Interpolation and Extrapolation: Estimating values between or beyond known data points, including:

Polynomial Interpolation: Fitting a polynomial to a set of data points.

Spline Interpolation: Using piecewise polynomials to create smoother interpolations.

Numerical Integration: Approximating definite integrals, including:

Trapezoidal Rule: Approximating the integral using trapezoids.

Simpson's Rule: Using quadratic polynomials for a more accurate approximation.

Monte Carlo Integration: Using random sampling to estimate the integral.

Numerical Differentiation: Approximating derivatives of functions, including:

Finite Difference Methods: Using finite differences to approximate derivatives.

Solving Ordinary Differential Equations (ODEs): Finding solutions to ODEs, including:

Euler's Method: A simple first-order method.

Runge-Kutta Methods: A family of higher-order methods for more accurate solutions.

Julia's Numerical Computing Ecosystem:

Standard Library: Exploring Julia's built-in functions for numerical methods, such as `roots`, `interp`, `quadgk`, and `diffeqsolve`.

Numerical Libraries: Introducing key packages for numerical computing, such as:

DifferentialEquations.jl: A comprehensive library for solving ODEs, partial differential equations (PDEs), and other differential equations.

Optim.jl: A library for optimization, including finding minima and maxima of functions.

LinearAlgebra.jl: A library for linear algebra operations, including solving linear systems and eigenvalue problems.

Advanced Topics:

Error Analysis: Understanding and quantifying the errors introduced by numerical approximations.

Stability and Convergence: Analyzing the stability and convergence properties of numerical methods.

Adaptive Methods: Using adaptive methods that adjust step sizes or parameters to achieve desired accuracy.

High-Performance Computing: Applying numerical methods in parallel or distributed environments for large-scale problems.

Practical Examples and Use Cases:

Modeling Physical Systems: Using numerical methods to simulate physical phenomena, such as projectile motion, pendulum oscillations, or heat transfer.

Financial Modeling: Applying numerical methods to solve financial problems, such as option pricing or portfolio optimization.

Data Analysis: Using numerical methods for data analysis tasks, such as curve fitting, interpolation, or numerical integration of data.

Machine Learning: Implementing numerical optimization algorithms for training machine learning models.

8.2 Differential Equations and Modeling

What are Differential Equations?

Definitions and Types: We'll start with a clear explanation of what differential equations (DEs) are, including:

Ordinary Differential Equations (ODEs): Equations involving a function of one independent variable and its derivatives.

Partial Differential Equations (PDEs): Equations involving a function of multiple independent variables and its partial derivatives.

Examples: Illustrating different types of DEs with examples from physics, engineering, biology, and economics.

Why Model with DEs?

Dynamic Systems: We'll explain that DEs are essential for modeling systems that change over time, such as:

Population Growth: Modeling how populations change over time due to birth, death, and migration.

Chemical Reactions: Describing the rates of change of chemical concentrations in a reaction.

Motion of Objects: Modeling the movement of objects under the influence of forces.

Spread of Diseases: Simulating how diseases spread through a population.

Building DE Models:

Identifying Variables: Guiding readers on how to identify the key variables and parameters that describe a system.

Formulating Equations: Translating relationships between variables into mathematical equations involving derivatives.

Initial and Boundary Conditions: Specifying initial or boundary conditions to define a specific solution to the DE.

Solving DEs in Julia:

DifferentialEquations.jl: Introducing DifferentialEquations.jl, a powerful Julia library for solving various types of DEs, including:

ODE Solvers: Exploring different numerical methods for solving ODEs, such as Runge-Kutta methods and adaptive solvers.

PDE Solvers: Discussing methods for solving PDEs, such as finite difference methods and finite element methods.

Symbolic Solutions: Using symbolic computation to find analytical solutions when possible.

Analyzing and Visualizing Solutions:

Interpreting Results: Guiding readers on how to interpret the solutions obtained from DE solvers and relate them back to the real-world system.

Visualization: Using plotting libraries like Plots.jl to visualize the solutions and gain insights into the system's behavior.

Sensitivity Analysis: Exploring how changes in parameters affect the solution, providing insights into the system's robustness and key factors.

Practical Examples and Use Cases:

Predator-Prey Models: Simulating the dynamics of predator-prey interactions using Lotka-Volterra equations.

Epidemic Modeling: Modeling the spread of infectious diseases using SIR (Susceptible-Infected-Recovered) models.

Chemical Kinetics: Simulating chemical reactions and analyzing reaction rates.

Financial Modeling: Using DEs to model stock prices, interest rates, or option pricing.

8.3 High-Performance Simulations

Why High-Performance Simulations?

Complexity: We'll start by emphasizing that many real-world simulations involve complex systems with numerous variables, interactions, and intricate dynamics. These simulations often require significant computational resources.

Scale: Simulations can involve large datasets, high resolutions, or long time scales, demanding efficient algorithms and parallel computing techniques.

Real-time Requirements: Some simulations, such as those used in interactive applications or real-time decision-making, require rapid execution and low latency.

Julia for High-Performance Simulations:

Performance: Reiterating Julia's speed advantages, which are crucial for achieving high performance in simulations.

Parallelism: Revisiting Julia's rich support for parallelism, including multithreading, distributed computing, and GPU programming.

Libraries and Tools: Showcasing Julia's ecosystem of packages for high-performance simulations, including DifferentialEquations.jl, Agents.jl, and CUDA.jl.

Techniques for High-Performance Simulations:

Algorithm Optimization: Exploring efficient algorithms and data structures for simulations, such as:

Spatial Data Structures: Using efficient data structures like octrees or k-d trees for spatial queries and interactions.

Numerical Methods: Employing optimized numerical methods for solving differential equations, performing integrations, or handling other mathematical operations.

Random Number Generation: Utilizing efficient random number generators for stochastic simulations.

Parallel Computing: Leveraging parallelism to accelerate simulations, including:

Multithreading: Distributing computations across multiple cores on a single machine.

Distributed Computing: Running simulations on a cluster of machines to handle large-scale problems.

GPU Acceleration: Utilizing GPUs for computationally intensive parts of the simulation.

Memory Management: Optimizing memory usage to reduce overhead and improve performance, such as:

Data Locality: Arranging data in memory to improve cache utilization.

Avoiding Allocations: Minimizing memory allocations to reduce garbage collection overhead.

Array Operations: Using efficient array operations and libraries like LoopVectorization.jl for optimized computations.

Simulation Frameworks and Tools:

DifferentialEquations.jl: Exploring advanced features of DifferentialEquations.jl for high-performance simulations of dynamic systems.

Agents.jl: Introducing Agents.jl for agent-based modeling and simulations, including parallel and distributed simulations.

CUDA.jl: Demonstrating how to use CUDA.jl to accelerate simulations on GPUs.

Profiling and Benchmarking: Using profiling tools to identify performance bottlenecks and benchmarking to measure improvements.

Practical Examples and Use Cases:

Climate Modeling: Simulating climate patterns and predicting future changes using high-performance computing.

Fluid Dynamics: Modeling fluid flow in various applications, such as aircraft design or weather forecasting, using parallel simulations.

Molecular Dynamics: Simulating the interactions of millions of atoms or molecules using GPU acceleration.

Astrophysics: Simulating the evolution of galaxies or the universe using distributed computing.

Epidemiology: Modeling the spread of diseases through large populations using agent-based simulations.

Chapter 9

Emerging Julia Frontiers

9.1 GPU Programming with Julia

Why GPUs for Julia?

Massive Parallelism: We'll start by explaining how GPUs excel at parallel processing, making them ideal for tasks that can be broken down into many smaller, independent operations.

Performance Boost: Highlighting the significant performance gains that can be achieved by offloading computations to GPUs, especially for tasks like matrix operations, image processing, and deep learning.

Julia's GPU Ecosystem: Introducing Julia's GPU programming ecosystem, including:

CUDA.jl: A package for programming NVIDIA GPUs using CUDA.

AMDGPU.jl: A package for programming AMD GPUs using ROCm.

GPUArrays.jl: An abstract array interface for working with arrays on GPUs.

GPU Programming Concepts:

GPU Architecture: We'll provide a basic overview of GPU architecture, including:

Streaming Multiprocessors (SMs): The core processing units within a GPU.

CUDA Cores: The individual processing elements within an SM.

Memory Hierarchy: The different levels of memory on a GPU, including global memory, shared memory, and registers.

Kernel Functions: Explaining how to write kernel functions, which are functions that execute on the GPU.

Data Transfer: Discussing how to transfer data between the CPU and GPU memory.

Synchronization: Addressing the importance of synchronization to ensure correct execution of parallel operations on the GPU.

GPU Programming with CUDA.jl:

Writing Kernels: Demonstrating how to define and launch kernel functions using CUDA.jl.

Memory Management: Explaining how to allocate and manage memory on the GPU using CUDA.jl.

Array Operations: Performing array operations on the GPU using CUDA.jl and GPUArrays.jl.

Example Applications: Implementing simple GPU-accelerated programs, such as matrix multiplication or image processing.

Advanced GPU Programming:

Optimization Techniques: Exploring techniques for optimizing GPU code, such as:

Memory Coalescing: Accessing memory efficiently to maximize bandwidth.

Shared Memory: Utilizing shared memory for faster data access within a thread block.

Warp Divergence: Minimizing warp divergence to improve performance.

Deep Learning with GPUs: Revisiting deep learning and demonstrating how to train deep learning models on GPUs using Flux.jl and CUDA.jl.

Other GPU Libraries: Briefly mentioning other GPU programming libraries in Julia, such as:

cuBLAS.jl: A wrapper for the CUDA BLAS library for linear algebra operations.

cuDNN.jl: A wrapper for the CUDA Deep Neural Network library for deep learning.

Practical Examples and Use Cases:

Image Processing: Accelerating image processing tasks, such as image filtering or object detection, using GPUs.

Scientific Simulations: Performing computationally intensive scientific simulations, such as fluid dynamics or molecular dynamics, on GPUs.

Financial Modeling: Accelerating financial simulations and risk analysis using GPUs.

Data Analysis: Performing large-scale data analysis tasks, such as matrix factorization or clustering, on GPUs.

9.2 Quantum Computing and Julia

What is Quantum Computing?

Quantum Mechanics: We'll start with a gentle introduction to the fundamental concepts of quantum mechanics, including:

Superposition: The ability of a quantum system to be in multiple states simultaneously.

Entanglement: The phenomenon where two or more quantum systems are linked together, even when separated by large distances.

Qubits: The basic unit of quantum information, analogous to bits in classical computing.

Quantum Computers: We'll explain how quantum computers leverage these quantum phenomena to perform computations in a fundamentally different way than classical computers.

Applications: We'll discuss potential applications of quantum computing, such as:

Drug Discovery: Simulating molecular interactions to design new drugs and therapies.

Materials Science: Developing new materials with improved properties.

Financial Modeling: Creating more accurate and efficient financial models.

Cryptography: Breaking existing encryption algorithms and developing new, quantum-resistant ones.

Julia for Quantum Computing:

Why Julia? We'll highlight Julia's advantages for quantum computing, including:

Performance: Julia's speed is crucial for simulating quantum systems and developing quantum algorithms.

Abstraction: Julia's high-level syntax allows for expressing quantum algorithms in a clear and concise way.

Ecosystem: Introducing Julia's growing ecosystem of packages for quantum computing, such as Yao.jl and QuantumOptics.jl.

Quantum Computing Libraries in Julia:

Yao.jl: We'll focus on Yao.jl, a powerful and extensible framework for quantum computing that provides:

Quantum Circuit Simulation: Simulating quantum circuits on classical computers.

Quantum Algorithm Design: Building and testing quantum algorithms.

Quantum Hardware Integration: Interfacing with real quantum computers.

Other Libraries: We'll mention other quantum computing libraries in Julia, such as:

QuantumOptics.jl: A library for simulating quantum optical systems.

PastaQ.jl: A library for simulating and benchmarking quantum computers using tensor networks.

Quantum Programming Concepts:

Qubits and Quantum Gates: Explaining how to represent qubits and quantum gates in Julia.

Quantum Circuits: Building quantum circuits using Yao.jl's block-based approach.

Measurements: Performing measurements on quantum states and interpreting the results.

Quantum Algorithms: Implementing basic quantum algorithms, such as Grover's search algorithm and Shor's factoring algorithm.

Advanced Quantum Computing:

Quantum Error Correction: Discussing techniques for mitigating errors in quantum computations.

Quantum Machine Learning: Exploring the intersection of quantum computing and machine learning.

Quantum Simulation: Simulating quantum systems to study their properties and behavior.

Quantum Hardware: Briefly overviewing different types of quantum computers and their capabilities.

Practical Examples and Use Cases:

Quantum Teleportation: Implementing a quantum teleportation protocol using Yao.jl.

Quantum Key Distribution: Developing a quantum key distribution protocol for secure communication.

Quantum Chemistry: Simulating molecular properties using quantum algorithms.

Optimization Problems: Solving optimization problems using quantum annealing or variational quantum algorithms.

9.3 The Future of the Julia Ecosystem

Current Trends and Developments:

Language Evolution: We'll start by discussing the ongoing development of the Julia language itself, including:

New Features: Highlighting recent and upcoming language features that enhance performance, expressiveness, and usability.

Compiler Improvements: Discussing ongoing efforts to improve the Julia compiler, such as optimizing code generation, reducing latency, and enhancing error messages.

Static Compilation: Exploring advancements in static compilation, which can further improve performance and enable new deployment scenarios.

Package Ecosystem Growth: Examining the rapid expansion of the Julia package ecosystem, including:

Key Packages: Showcasing new and noteworthy packages in various domains, such as machine learning, data science, scientific computing, and web development.

Package Quality and Maintenance: Discussing initiatives to improve package quality, documentation, and maintenance to ensure a robust and reliable ecosystem.

Interoperability: Highlighting efforts to improve interoperability with other languages and tools, expanding Julia's reach and versatility.

Emerging Areas and Applications:

Artificial Intelligence (AI): Exploring Julia's growing role in AI, including:

Deep Learning: Discussing advancements in deep learning frameworks and libraries, such as Flux.jl and Knet.jl.

Machine Learning: Showcasing new machine learning algorithms and tools available in Julia.

AI for Science: Highlighting how Julia is being used to accelerate scientific discovery in fields like drug discovery, materials science, and climate modeling.

High-Performance Computing (HPC): Examining Julia's increasing adoption in HPC, including:

Parallel and Distributed Computing: Discussing new tools and techniques for parallel and distributed computing in Julia.

GPU Computing: Exploring advancements in GPU programming with Julia.

Scientific Simulations: Showcasing how Julia is being used for large-scale scientific simulations.

Web Development: Discussing the growing use of Julia for web development, including:

Web Frameworks: Highlighting new and improved web frameworks, such as Genie.jl and Dash.jl.

API Development: Building APIs and web services using Julia.

Interactive Applications: Creating interactive web applications and dashboards with Julia.

Community and Collaboration:

Julia Community: Emphasizing the importance of the Julia community in driving the language's growth and success.

Open Source Contributions: Encouraging readers to contribute to the Julia ecosystem by developing packages, improving documentation, or participating in discussions.

JuliaCon and Other Events: Highlighting JuliaCon and other community events that foster collaboration and knowledge sharing.

Challenges and Opportunities:

Challenges: Addressing challenges that the Julia ecosystem faces, such as improving package discoverability, attracting more developers, and ensuring long-term sustainability.

Opportunities: Discussing opportunities for growth and innovation, such as expanding into new application domains, improving tooling and infrastructure, and promoting Julia's adoption in industry and academia.

Chapter 10

Julia Community and Resources

10.1 Contributing to Open-Source Projects

Why Contribute to Open Source?

Giving Back: We'll start by emphasizing the collaborative spirit of open source and how contributing is a way to give back to the community that has built the tools and resources we use.

Skill Development: Contributing to open-source projects is an excellent way to improve programming skills, learn new technologies, and gain real-world experience.

Community Engagement: Participating in open-source projects allows you to connect with other developers, learn from experienced contributors, and build valuable relationships.

Impact: Your contributions can have a real impact on the projects you contribute to, making them better for everyone.

Finding Projects to Contribute To:

JuliaHub: We'll introduce JuliaHub as a central platform for discovering Julia packages and projects.

GitHub: Explaining how to find Julia projects on GitHub and explore their code, issues, and contribution guidelines.

Community Forums: Mentioning online forums and communities where developers discuss Julia and open-source projects.

Interests and Skills: Encouraging readers to find projects that align with their interests and skills, making contributions more enjoyable and effective.

Types of Contributions:

Code Contributions: Discussing different ways to contribute code, such as:

Bug Fixes: Identifying and fixing bugs or issues in the code.

New Features: Implementing new features or enhancements.

Performance Improvements: Optimizing code for better performance.

Refactoring: Improving code structure and readability.

Non-Code Contributions: Highlighting that valuable contributions can also be made without writing code, such as:

Documentation: Improving documentation, writing tutorials, or translating existing materials.

Testing: Testing code, reporting bugs, and providing feedback.

Community Support: Answering questions, helping others, and participating in discussions.

How to Contribute:

Forking and Cloning: Explaining how to fork a repository on GitHub and clone it to your local machine.

Creating Branches: Creating new branches for your contributions to keep your changes organized.

Making Changes: Making changes to the code or documentation.

Committing and Pushing: Committing your changes with clear messages and pushing them to your forked repository.

Submitting Pull Requests: Creating pull requests to propose your changes to the original project.

Best Practices for Contributing:

Communication: Communicating clearly and respectfully with other contributors.

Coding Style: Following the project's coding style guidelines to ensure consistency.

Testing: Testing your changes thoroughly before submitting them.

Documentation: Documenting your code and any changes you make.

Respecting Community Decisions: Understanding that project maintainers have the final say on whether to accept contributions.

Contributing to the Julia Language Itself:

Julia Development: Briefly mentioning how readers can contribute to the development of the Julia language itself by participating in discussions, proposing new features, or contributing to the compiler.

10.2 Finding Help and Support

Julia's Supportive Community

Open and Welcoming: We'll start by emphasizing the welcoming and inclusive nature of the Julia community. Help is readily available for users of all levels, from beginners to experts.

Diverse Channels: Highlighting the various channels where support can be found:

Discourse Forum: The official Julia Discourse forum is a central hub for discussions, questions, and announcements.

Slack: The Julia Slack community provides real-time chat and collaboration.

GitHub: Julia repositories on GitHub are a great place to report issues, ask questions, and engage with developers.

Stack Overflow: The Julia tag on Stack Overflow is a valuable resource for finding answers to common questions.

Local Meetups and JuliaCon: Mentioning local meetups and the annual JuliaCon conference as opportunities to connect with other Julia users and learn from experts.

Effective Help-Seeking Strategies:

Asking Good Questions: Providing tips on how to ask clear and concise questions that are more likely to get helpful answers, including:

Providing Context: Explaining the problem clearly and providing relevant code snippets or error messages.

Searching Existing Resources: Checking if the question has already been answered in documentation or online forums.

Being Specific: Focusing on a specific issue rather than asking broad or vague questions.

Showing Effort: Demonstrating that you've already tried to solve the problem yourself.

Using Documentation Effectively: Emphasizing the importance of consulting the official Julia documentation and package documentation for information and examples.

Debugging Techniques: Revisiting debugging techniques and tools that can help identify and resolve issues independently.

Resources for Different Needs:

Beginners: Pointing to resources specifically designed for beginners, such as tutorials, introductory books, and online courses.

Intermediate Users: Recommending resources for intermediate users, such as advanced documentation, specialized packages, and community forums.

Advanced Users: Highlighting resources for advanced users, such as contributing to open-source projects, participating in language development, and engaging in research.

Building a Support Network:

Mentorship: Suggesting seeking out mentors or experienced Julia users who can provide guidance and support.

Collaboration: Encouraging collaboration with other Julia users on projects or learning initiatives.

Giving Back: Highlighting that helping others is also a great way to learn and solidify one's understanding of Julia.

10.3 Staying Up-to-Date with Julia's Evolution

Keeping Pace with a Dynamic Language

The Importance of Staying Current: We'll start by highlighting why it's crucial to stay up-to-date with Julia's evolution, including:

New Features and Improvements: Taking advantage of new language features, performance enhancements, and bug fixes.

Package Updates: Keeping packages updated to benefit from the latest improvements and security fixes.

Community Engagement: Staying connected with the Julia community to learn about new developments and best practices.

Enhanced Skills: Continuously learning and expanding your Julia knowledge and skills.

Channels for Staying Informed:

Official Julia Blog: Following the official Julia blog for announcements of new releases, features, and events.

Discourse Forum: Participating in the Julia Discourse forum to engage in discussions, ask questions, and learn from others.

JuliaLang Twitter: Following the official Julia language Twitter account for news and updates.

JuliaCon: Attending JuliaCon, the annual Julia conference, to learn about the latest developments and connect with the community.

Newsletters and Blogs: Subscribing to Julia newsletters or following blogs that cover Julia news and developments.

GitHub: Watching Julia repositories on GitHub to track changes and new releases.

Managing Updates:

Keeping Julia Up-to-Date: Using the `julia` REPL to update to the latest stable release of Julia.

Updating Packages: Using the `Pkg` REPL mode to update packages to their latest versions.

Managing Environments: Creating and managing separate environments to isolate project dependencies and avoid conflicts.

Learning Resources:

Julia Documentation: Referring to the official Julia documentation, which is regularly updated with new information and examples.

Online Courses and Tutorials: Taking advantage of online courses and tutorials that cover the latest Julia features and best practices.

Books and Publications: Staying current with new books and publications on Julia.

Community Forums: Engaging in discussions and asking questions on community forums to learn from others.

Contributing to Julia's Evolution:

Providing Feedback: Sharing feedback on new features, language changes, and documentation to help shape the future of Julia.

Reporting Bugs: Reporting bugs and issues to help improve the stability and reliability of Julia.

Contributing to Open-Source Projects: Contributing to the development of Julia packages and libraries to enhance the ecosystem.

Participating in Discussions: Engaging in discussions on language design and development to contribute to the evolution of Julia.

www.ingramcontent.com/pod-product-compliance
Lightning Source LLC
LaVergne TN
LVHW012320060326
832904LV00028B/342